Tell me...

WHY DIDN'T MUMMIES HAVE BRAINS?

...and more about history

CHRYSALIS CHILDREN'S BOOKS

First published in the UK in 2003 by
Chrysalis Children's Books PLC,
64 Brewery Road,
London N7 9NT

A ZIGZAG BOOK

British Library Cataloguing in Publication Data for this book is available from the British Library.

Every effort has been made to ensure that none of the recommended websites in this book is linked to inappropriate material. However, due to the nature of the Internet, the publishers regret that they cannot take responsibility for future content of the websites.

Produced by Miles Kelly Publishing Ltd
Bardfield Centre, Great Bardfield, Essex CM7 4SL

Editorial Director: Anne Marshall
Editor: Mark Darling
Copy Editor: Sarah Ridley
Indexer: Jane Parker
Proofreader: Hayley Kerr, Leon Gray
Designer: Michelle Cannatella
Artwork Commissioning: Bethany Walker

Editorial Director, Chrysalis Children's Books: Honor Head

ISBN: 1 903954 92 4

Printed and bound in Malaysia

Contents

Make-its

Pyramid cakes 7

Make a Viking arm-ring 17

Maya and Aztec books 21

Design a flag 27

Where did the first humans live?

Most scientists think that the first modern humans (scientific name: *Homo sapiens sapiens*) lived in East Africa around 200,000BC. Like us, they could talk, hunt and use fire. Around 125,000BC groups of these early humans began to leave Africa. Gradually, they settled all around the world.

A beginning

- The world's first known pottery came from Japan, around 9000BC. Before that, people stored food in baskets woven from grass, or leather pouches.
- All our pet dogs are descended from wolves, tamed by prehistoric people living around 10,500 years ago.

INTERNET LINK
Discover the secrets of Stonehenge
http://library.thinkquest.org/CR0211481
/Stonehenge/stonehenge.htm

⊕ Why did farming change the world for ever?

Around 8500BC, the climate in the Middle East changed and became very dry. People had to live close to rivers or streams. Hunters could no longer go far in search of food, so they gathered wild grass seeds that grew close-by, and stored them to eat later. They noticed how seeds they dropped grew into new plants. So they scattered more, and harvested them. They had invented farming and a settled way of life.

QUICK QUIZ
1. In which English county can you find Stonehenge?
2. In what countries can you find pictures painted underground on the walls of caves?
3. On which of the world's three continents have Homo sapiens fossils been discovered?

....

Answers — see page 32.

⊕ Was this the world's biggest clock?

Stonehenge is a massive stone monument in southern England, built between 3000 and 1500BC. No one knows exactly why it was made. It might have been a temple for worshipping sky-gods, or an observatory where priests calculated time by watching the movements of the Sun.

⊕ Who had front doors in their roofs?

The farmers, traders and craftworkers from Çatal Hüyük in Turkey lived in houses with rooftop doorways. Çatal Hüyük, one of the world's first cities, was built around 9,000 years ago. Its houses were tightly packed together. There were no streets or pavements, but walkways across the roofs. Visitors entered at roof level and climbed down a ladder to reach the rooms inside.

Why didn't mummies have brains?

Because mummy-makers removed them! After an Egyptian died, the body was taken to a workshop called 'the beautiful house'. All the body's inner organs, including the brain, were removed to stop the body rotting. Then the muscles, skin and bones were left for weeks in natron (rather like salt) to dry them out. Finally, they were wrapped up in linen bandages and laid in a decorated case.

INTERNET LINK

For all you need to know about ancient Egypt
www.ancientegypt.co.uk/menu.html

Find out why you wouldn't want to be a mummy!
www.salariya.com/web_books/mummy/

▶ *Mummy-makers placed magic amulets and lucky charms in-between layers of bandages to protect the dead body inside.*

6

↑ What contains 3,200,000 blocks of stone?

The Great Pyramid at Giza in Egypt – the most famous pyramid in the world. It is 148 metres tall, and its base is 230 metres square. Each stone block weighs about 2½ tonnes! It took 100,000 men 23 years to build. The Great Pyramid is the tomb of Pharaoh Khufu, who died in 2566BC. For the ancient Egyptians, its shape had magic meanings. Its height linked Earth with heaven. Its sloping sides were like the Sun's life-giving rays, and its top was like the first land – a mighty mountain that rose from the sea.

Egyptian times

● Until the 20th century, dried flesh from Egyptian mummies was eaten as a medicine, and crushed to make fertiliser to use on the fields.

● Egyptian pyramids have lasted for over 4,000 years. But now pollution from fires, factories and traffic fumes is damaging their stones.

Pyramid cakes

You will need:
2 egg whites, 100 grams sugar, 175 grams desiccated coconut, egg whisk or electric beater, baking sheet, a little margarine

1. Whisk the egg whites and sugar together until just frothy. Stir in the coconut.

2. Grease the baking sheet with a little margarine.

3. Place spoonfuls of the coconut mixture on the baking sheet. Make each into a pyramid shape.

4. Cook in the oven at 170°C/Gas Mark 3 for about 35 minutes.

Our word 'pyramid' comes from 'pyramis' – a mound-shaped cake that was popular in ancient Greece. This modern recipe makes eight pyramid cakes.

← Who welcomed floods?

Egyptians who lived on the banks of the River Nile waited for it to flood their fields each year. The life-giving water and rich silt – tiny particles of soil, decaying plants and manure – helped Egyptian farmers' crops to grow.

Which city was 'the home of democracy'?

Democracy means government by the people, and many governments all round the world are run as democracies today. Democracy was invented in the powerful Greek city-state of Athens over 2,500 years ago. Athenian citizens met in an assembly to discuss politics, elect leaders and make new laws. Young men, women, foreigners and slaves could not take part.

▼ *All adult male citizens could join in democratic debates in Athens. Each speech was carefully timed to make sure it was not too long.*

Where did Greeks dare to be bare?

At the Olympic Games, and at other sports festivals, athletes often competed with no clothes on! There were two reasons for this. First, Greek clothes were loose and flowing and they got in the way when athletes ran. Second, Greek people admired fit, healthy bodies, and liked to display them. Prize-winning athletes acted as naked models for Greek artists, who carved statues of them in stone.

Why did hungry Greeks look forward to festivals?

Because they could share in the feast! On religious festival days, Greek priests sacrificed animals to gods and goddesses on altars in front of temples. The meat from each sacrificed animal was roasted and shared among worshippers. The gods got the skin and the bones.

What a state!

- Greece was divided into many city states – big towns with the land around them.
- Greek civilisation reached its peak around 600–200BC, but its influence lives on. We still use Greek words (such as 'mega' and 'economy'), study Greek scientists and thinkers and admire Greek art.

INTERNET LINK
Learn all about ancient Greece
www.bbc.co.uk/schools/landmarks/ancientgreece
/main_menu.shtml

Who wanted to conquer the world?

King Alexander III of Macedon (a state on the northern frontiers of Greece) aimed to rule the world. Better known as Alexander the Great, he became king in 337BC at the age of 20. His army conquered a vast empire, stretching from Egypt to Afghanistan. Alexander wanted to go further and conquer India, but his soldiers were homesick and forced him to turn back.

Where was the world's first shopping mall?

The first big shopping street was Trajan's Market in the great city of Rome. Trajan (ruled AD98–117) was the emperor who paid for it to be built. It contained 150 shops and offices on five levels and a huge central hall. It stood close to the Roman Forum, the centre of Roman government, a large open square at the heart of the city, surrounded by temples, law courts and grand monuments. Public meetings were held in the Forum, and citizens met to exchange news and views and argue about politics. Ruins of some of these buildings can be seen today.

Rich Romans

- The city of Rome began as a few huts on a hillside around 1000BC. By around 300BC, the Romans ruled all Italy and began to conquer neighbouring lands.
- The government of Rome feared that its citizens might riot. So it kept them happy with 'bread and circuses' – handouts of food and free entertainment.

▼ *Statues of famous heroes were placed in the Roman Forum to inspire passers-by.*

⬆ Who wrote home to ask for woolly socks?

Letters have survived written by Roman soldiers guarding Hadrian's Wall, including one asking for socks! Hadrian's Wall is a strong stone barrier, 117 kilometres long, that marked the northern edge of the Roman Empire. It was built around AD122 in bleak, windswept country in northern England, where it often snowed. The soldiers must have found it very chilly!

⬊ Who was frightened of a warrior's wife?

The Romans were really frightened of Queen Boudicca. When the Romans invaded England, the Celtic people were already there. Celtic men were known as brave fighters, but it was Boudicca who really fought back. In AD60, she led a rebellion. Her armies destroyed three cities and killed around 50,000 Romans and their friends. Eventually, the Roman army defeated the rebels.

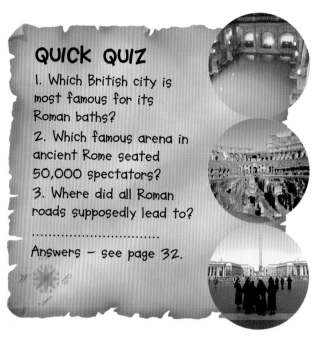

QUICK QUIZ
1. Which British city is most famous for its Roman baths?
2. Which famous arena in ancient Rome seated 50,000 spectators?
3. Where did all Roman roads supposedly lead to?
....
Answers – see page 32.

INTERNET LINK
Have fun discovering ancient Rome
www.bbc.co.uk/schools/romans/

⬊ How often did Romans have a bath?

Wealthy families bathed every day in their own private bathhouses, with piped hot water, or at the public baths. Other Romans rinsed their hands and faces in a bowl of cold water each morning. To get really clean they went to the public baths, which they did once every nine days.

What was the biggest grave in the world?

The Great Wall of China became a giant grave for many of the workers who built it, because the work was so hard. Those workers who dropped dead were buried inside. The Great Wall was built for Shi Huangdi to protect his empire. Work on the Great Wall began around 210BC. When finished, it stretched for 6,700 kilometres. Thousands of Chinese men were forced to leave their homes and farms to build it.

▲ *Guards kept watch for invaders from look-out posts built all along the Wall.*

▼ *The Great Wall of China was built of pounded earth and protected by a strong stone casing.*

INTERNET LINK
All about the Great Wall of China
EnchantedLearning.com/subjects/greatwall
/Allabout.html

12

⊙ Who buried a model army?

Shi Huangdi, the first Chinese Emperor, (259–210BC) built a huge tomb, full of everything he would need in the afterlife, including thousands of life-size terracotta (baked clay) warriors to guard it. In this way, he hoped to hold on to power after his death. The men who designed and built the tomb were killed and buried inside, so they could not give its secrets away.

⊙ How did 'Marco the Millions' get his name?

Italian merchant Marco Polo (1254–1324) returned with rich treasures from his long, dangerous journey to China. He was away from home for 20 years. When he returned, with strange stories about the splendid Chinese civilisation, some people did not believe him. They accused Marco Polo of boasting or inventing his fantastic tales.

⊙ Whose power was always hidden?

Japanese people believed that their royal family was too special to be seen by ordinary men and women. According to legends, they were descended from the Sun Goddess. With their courtiers and bodyguards, they lived shut away from the rest of the world, in a beautiful palace surrounded by lovely gardens.

Which soldiers built towers of skulls?

Soldiers in the army led by the famous Mongol emperor Genghis Khan (1162–1227) lived in tents of wool felt, called yurts. The Mongols were nomads, and moved from place to place. Between 1200 and 1300, Mongol troops conquered a vast empire, stretching from eastern China to central Europe. They built grim skull-towers with the heads of their enemies to celebrate battle victories.

▲ This beautiful tomb in India – the Taj Mahal – was built in 1648 by Mughal Emperor Shah Jahan for his favourite wife. The Mughals were descended from Mongol warlords who conquered India in 1526.

◀ Mongol families travelled with flocks of sheep and goats, which provided meat, milk, leather and wool.

→ How did one city change the world?

Mecca in Arabia was home to the Prophet Muhammad (AD571–632). He received messages from God and began to tell his fellow citizens about them. Some people welcomed his preaching. They became known as Muslims – people who submit to God. But others hated his preaching, and in AD622 they drove Muhammad out of the city. He returned in AD630, and the citizens of Mecca accepted the Muslim faith. Soon, it spread to many parts of the world.

INTERNET LINK

For a look into the world of the Mongols
www.geocities.com/Athens/Forum/2532/

Star scholars

- Early Muslim scholars were great scientists and astronomers. They gave many stars and constellations the names we still use today.
- When Genghis Khan died his body was carried thousands of kilometres to be buried close to his home in Mongolia. Every person, animal or bird it passed was killed, so that its spirit could serve him in the next world.

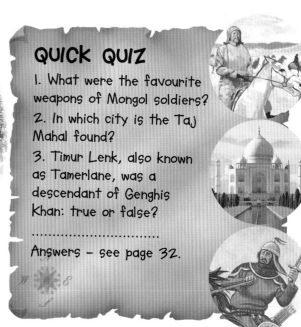

QUICK QUIZ

1. What were the favourite weapons of Mongol soldiers?
2. In which city is the Taj Mahal found?
3. Timur Lenk, also known as Tamerlane, was a descendant of Genghis Khan: true or false?
....
Answers – see page 32.

↓ Who was buried in a blue tomb?

Mongol warlord Timur Lenk, who ruled the great trading city of Samarkand in Central Asia from 1369 to 1405, was buried there. He plundered many rich cities in northern India and the Middle East. Although fierce and bloodthirsty, he admired all the arts. He was buried in a tomb covered with tiles that glowed green and blue in the sunlight.

Why did the Vikings set sail?

For many reasons! Some historians say that Vikings had used up all the good farmland in their home countries – Norway, Sweden and Denmark. Some say that they travelled to buy and sell things, then moved to live closer to good markets. Others say that they just liked raiding and conquering new lands!

Viking violence

- The Vikings were most powerful between AD800 and 1100. After that they weakened, and Viking lands were divided into three separate states.
- The Vikings settled in Iceland, Greenland, Scotland, Ireland, eastern England, Russia and France.

▼ *Viking raiders sailed their shallow-hulled longships right up to shore, making surprise attacks on coastal villages, farms and churches.*

→ Where did East meet West?

Traders, scholars and artists came to the fabulous city of Byzantium (modern Istanbul in Turkey) from China, the Middle East, North Africa, Russia and Western Europe. From AD330, Byzantium ruled half of the Roman Empire. As Roman power faded away, it became the centre of a rich, multi-cultural empire that lasted until AD1453.

▲ **Byzantine artists created this beautiful mosaic portrait of Empress Theodora, who ruled in the 6th century AD. It is made from tiny fragments of coloured pottery, gold leaf and glass.**

INTERNET LINK
Find out all about the Vikings
www.bbc.co.uk/education/vikings/index.shtml

↑ How did Greenland get its name?

It was given its name by Viking explorer Erik the Red, who settled there around AD983. To encourage others to join his new settlement he named it *green* – the colour of fields and trees. This was a cruel trick, since many Viking settlers died from cold and hunger. Most of the year round, Greenland is covered in snow and ice.

Make a Viking arm-ring

Viking kings rewarded brave warriors with heavy arm-rings made of silver and often shaped like dragons or snakes.

You will need:
thin card, scissors, cooking foil, glue, ballpoint pen, sticky tape

1. Cut a strip of card about 5 centimetres wide and long enough to fit comfortably around your upper arm, plus about 10 centimetres overlap. Cut a strip of foil big enough to cover the card.

2. Spread glue on one side of the card strip, and cover it neatly with foil.

3. When the glue is dry, turn the strip over so that the card side is uppermost.

4. Draw a pattern of snakes or dragons on the card. Press hard, so your design shows through on the foil side.

5. Use sticky tape to join the ends of your arm-ring.

Whose lives were tied to the land?

During the Middle Ages, many ordinary people were not free to take a job where they liked. They belonged to rich nobles, who had been given large estates by kings and queens. These peasants were allowed to live in small cottages and grow food in shared fields. But in return they had to work without pay on their lord's land. They also had to pay taxes and could not travel, bake bread, brew ale – or even get married – without his permission.

▼ Everyone worked together to harvest corn in medieval times. If the crop was damaged by rain or eaten by birds, they would starve.

⟳ Why were castles built?

To protect the land kings and lords had won in battle. They kept their families and servants safe and showed their power to other rich people. The first castles were built around AD900, and were made of wood. Later, from around AD1000, castles began to be made of stone, and were surrounded by strong stone walls. There was room inside for a whole community.

A knight's tale

● Knights stopped building castles when armies started using gunpowder, around 1450. Castle walls were easily smashed by stones and iron balls fired from a cannon.

● The children's rhyme 'Ring-a-Roses' probably describes an outbreak of plague long ago. Its final words – 'all fall down' – tell how plague victims died.

→ How did fleas spread a killer disease?

Fleas lived on diseased rats that carried the deadly plague. By biting the rats and sucking up their germ-filled blood, fleas spread the plague. For then they bit people and injected rat blood and germs with each bite. The germs grew inside human blood, and flea-bitten people fell ill with huge boils, fevers, coughs and bleeding. Most of them died.

⟲ What were 'sermons in stone'?

Huge cathedrals built by expert builders in European cities and towns between AD1000 and 1500 were described this way. Their painted walls and stained-glass windows carried pictures from Bible stories. They helped people who could not read (which meant most people) to learn about the Christian faith.

INTERNET LINK
What's it like inside a castle?
www.castles.org/Kids_Section/Castle_Story/

Who buried bodies in bundles?

Inca people in the high Andes Mountains of Peru wrapped the dead bodies of important people in cloth decorated with magic patterns. Then they buried them in cold caves or dry desert sand to preserve them. Once a year, in November, the mummified bodies of dead Inca emperors were carried through the streets in religious processions.

▲ *The mask of the Maya king, Pacal, who ruled the city-state of Palenque, Mexico, in the 9th century* AD.

INTERNET LINK
Travel through the history of the Aztecs
home.freeuk.net/elloughton13/mexico.htm

→ Who built gardens in the middle of a lake?

The Aztecs, who lived in Mexico, built their capital city on an island in a lake. All around they created *chinampas* (floating gardens) on rafts made of tree-branches, stones and mud, where they grew maize, beans, vegetables and flowers. They fertilised these crops with human manure collected from public lavatories built alongside busy roads.

Maya and Aztec books

You will need:
strip of paper about 10 x 40 centimetres, ruler, pen or pencil, felt-tip pens, paints and brush or crayons. You will also need to think of a story you can tell in pictures.

1. Make three small marks along the top of the paper strip. Leave 10 centimetres between each mark.

2. Use the marks to tell you where to fold the paper, like this.

3. Now think of a story you can tell in pictures. Draw it on the paper. Aztec stories often started at the bottom of the page and were read by zig-zagging up the lines of pictures to the top.

Maya and Aztec books were made in the same way. They were folded like a concertina from long strips of paper, tree-bark or deerskin.

Masks and mummies

- The Maya ruled Mexico from around AD300–900. They built great cities and huge pyramid tombs. No one knows why their civilisation disappeared.
- Maya, Aztec and Inca people all offered sacrifices to please their gods. The Maya gave drops of blood, the Inca gave food, flowers and incense, but the Aztecs offered human hearts!

→ What did the Americas give us?

Chocolate, potatoes and tomatoes are some of today's most popular foods and drinks that originated in North and South America. They were unknown elsewhere in the world until 16th-century explorers brought them back to Europe, Africa and the Middle East. Pineapples, sunflowers, red peppers, avocados, hairless dogs (eaten by the Aztecs) and guinea pigs all came to Europe from the Americas!

How did a servant wreck a city?

In September 1666 a servant working for a baker in Pudding Lane, London, went to bed without putting a safety cover over the hearth. Sparks from the fire set light to the house, and soon whole streets nearby were aflame. The flames were fanned by a strong wind and raged out of control for five days. Over 13,000 homes were destroyed, as well as 87 churches and a cathedral.

London's burning

- For weeks after the Great Fire many of the surviving buildings continued to collapse as they cooled down.
- We know about the Great Fire of London because two famous writers, Samuel Pepys and John Evelyn, described it in their diaries, which still survive today.

⬅ Which woman said 'I have the heart and stomach of a man'?

Queen Elizabeth I made a rousing speech, including these words, to the soldiers waiting to repel the Spanish invasion in 1588. She said that she might not be as strong as a man, but she was just as brave as any king! In fact the Spanish Armada was defeated by the English Navy, so the soldiers did not have to fight.

INTERNET LINK

Learn all about the Tudor and Elizabethan times
www.snaithprimary.eril.net/tudors.htm

QUICK QUIZ

1. Which famous landmark, destroyed in the Great Fire, was redesigned by Sir Christopher Wren?
2. Which Tudor king had six wives?
3. Who created the Church of England?

....

Answers – see page 32.

⬇ Whose greed for gold changed the world forever?

European pirates and explorers, who set off on long expeditions in fragile sailing ships to hunt for spices, precious stones and distant lands, mapped the world. In 1521, a ship belonging to Portuguese explorer Ferdinand Magellan became the first to sail right round the world – though Magellan himself was killed before he reached home. In 1580, English adventurer Sir Francis Drake became the first man to sail round the world and survive.

Christopher Columbus

Sir Francis Drake

James Cook *Ferdinand Magellan*

Why did these pilgrims seek a new land?

They sailed away to find religious freedom. In 1620, a group of 102 people who had strong religious beliefs left Europe on board the ship *The Mayflower*. They hoped to set up a new community in America, to be run according to their Protestant views. The voyage was dangerous and half the settlers died during the first winter. The survivors were helped by friendly Native Americans.

A new world

- After Columbus sailed across the Atlantic Ocean in 1492, many European merchants and explorers went to North and South America, hoping to win fame and make their fortune.
- For almost 200 years, Britain, Spain, France and Portugal claimed the right to rule North and South America.

Who built homes without wood, bricks or stones?

European settlers on the Great Plains of North America used slabs of earth and turf, called 'sods', to build simple, single-storey farmhouses. Sod houses were often cold and damp – and could be dangerous. Heavy rain might cause the roof to collapse or the walls to crumble away. They were forced to use sods because no trees grew on the Plains, and they could not find clay to make bricks or building stone.

INTERNET LINK

Find out all about the first Americans
www.germantown.k12.il.us/html/intro.html

Who danced with ghosts to save their homes?

During the 1800s, European settlers in the United States drove Native American families away from their homelands, and forced them to settle on reservations (land set aside for them). Native Americans fought the settlers with guns. They also took part in religious dances, asking the ghosts of their dead ancestors to help them win back their homes. After dancing, some 'ghost warriors' believed they could not be killed in battle. Tragically, they were wrong.

Where would you meet an 'iron horse'?

This name was the nickname for steam-powered locomotives that revolutionised transport in the United States. Nearly 34,000 kilometres of new railway track were built between 1850 and 1860.

How many lost their heads in France?

About 17,000 people, including the king and queen, were executed during the French Revolution between 1789 and 1795. It began as a mass protest against the French government's unfair laws and taxes. When it ended, the whole of French life had changed. There were new laws, new government assemblies, a new flag and even new clothing styles.

▼ On 14 July 1789, angry crowds of French people attacked a royal palace in Paris. This marked the start of the French Revolution. In France today, 14 July is still a national holiday.

➡ Who declared war on big business?

The Bolsheviks, who led the Russian Revolution in 1917. They wanted to get rid of all kings, nobles, landowners and businesses, and give power to ordinary people. They shot the Russian Tsar (ruler) and his family, and set up a new, Communist government. Ordinary people ran the country and worked for the state instead of making money for themselves.

▲ **Nicholas II, the last Russian Tsar, and his family were all murdered by Communists in 1918.**

⬆ Who opened the door and set slaves free?

Afro-Caribbean slave Pierre Toussaint L'Ouverture (1743–1803) led a rebellion against slave-owners on the island of Haiti. By 1793, all slaves on Haiti were free. Toussaint's determination and bravery inspired other slave protests in the Caribbean and South America. Toussaint himself was captured by the French rulers, sent to France, and put in prison, where he died.

It's revolting

- The late 18th century was a time of revolutions in America, France, parts of South America and Ireland.
- During the 19th century, many small European countries, such as Greece and Italy, were ruled by larger, stronger ones, such as Austria-Hungary. They started wars to break free.

INTERNET LINK

Discover what caused the French Revolution
www.mcdougallittell.com/whist/netact
/U5/U5main.htm

Design a flag

You will need: paper, coloured pens, glue.

1. Design a flag on a piece of paper.

2. Cut out a large piece of paper the same shape as your flag.

3. Cut out pieces of paper to make up the different parts of your flag. Colour them and glue them to your flag.

Do you support a cause? Communist rebels in Russia carried a red flag decorated with a hammer and sickle (a big knife used to cut corn). Red was the colour of blood and passion. The hammer stood for factory workers, and the sickle stood for farmers.

Where was 'the workshop of the world'?

▼ Factories in the 19th century were noisy, dirty, crowded and very dangerous.

Between 1800 and 1900, British engineers and business people were the world leaders in technology and manufacturing. They invented huge steam-powered pumps, weaving looms, hammers and machine-tools to mass-produce goods in factories. They also built steam-powered ships and locomotives to transport their goods and inventions to many distant lands.

Machine power

- The years from 1750 to 1850 are often called the Industrial Revolution. Before then, people made everything they needed at home by hand, or bought them from workshops.
- After steam power was invented, most goods were mass-produced quickly in factories by machines.

← Who was 'the Grandmother of Europe'?

Queen Victoria – by the time she died, her children and grandchildren ruled in Denmark, Greece, Russia, Prussia and other German states and, of course, Britain, too. Queen Victoria reigned from 1837 to 1901 and had nine children with her German husband, Prince Albert. Because Britain and Germany were so powerful, royal families throughout Europe arranged marriages with them.

QUICK QUIZ

1. Which of these were invented in the 19th century: steam trains, bicycles, telephones or electric lights?
2. Which brothers built the first successful plane?
3. Which country was called the 'Jewel in the British Queen's Crown'?

....

Answers – see page 32.

⊙ Whose book shook the world?

In 1859, after many years of travel and study, British scientist Charles Darwin (1809–82) published his book *On the Origin of Species*. It shocked many readers. In it, Darwin put forward his view that living things evolve (change and develop) over time. In 1871, he had another book published, called *The Descent of Man*. In that, he claimed that humans were descended from wild creatures – probably apes. This book was also criticised and discussed by many people.

▶ **African colonies ruled by European states.**

French
British
Portuguese
German
Belgian
Italian
Spanish
Independent

↗ What was 'the scramble for Africa'?

Countries in Europe greedily scrambled to take control of lands in Africa during the second half of the 19th century. By 1900 many countries ruled colonies (areas of land) in Africa. They brought their own laws, languages and religion, and set up their own governments.

INTERNET LINK

Learn all about the Victorians
www.snaithprimary.eril.net/victoria.htm
What was life like for Victorian children?
www.bbc.co.uk/schools/victorians/standard/index.shtml

Which was 'the war to end all wars'?

The First World War (1914–18), was supposed to be. It was fought by Britain, France, Russia, the United States and their allies against Germany and its allies. Soldiers on both sides fought in terrible conditions. Over ten million men were killed. Their suffering was so terrible that politicians vowed war must never happen again. But just 21 years later, European nations – and their allies – were fighting the Second World War.

▲ *Suffragettes (British women protesting for the right to vote) often clashed with police between 1903 and 1913.*

▸ *Soldiers suffered appalling conditions in the trenches during the First World War.*

↓ Who made 'one small step'?

American astronaut Neil Armstrong (born in 1930) became the first man ever to land on the Moon in 1969. He set foot on the surface of the Moon with the carefully-planned words, 'That's one small step for a man, one giant leap for mankind.' The Moon landing came towards the end of a period of time known as the Space Race (from around 1957 to 1975), when the United States and the former Soviet Union tried to out-do each other's achievements.

QUICK QUIZ

1. Which First World War battle caused more than a million casualties?
2. Who first demonstrated television in 1925?
3. When did an astronaut last walk on the Moon?

....
Answers – see page 32.

◄ *Apollo Moon landings (1969–72)*

▲ **Gemini (1965–66)**

▲ *Space shuttle (1981–present)*

▲ *International space station (1998–present)*

The modern world

- Computer, supermarkets, takeaway food, jet planes and television were all invented after 1900.
- Teenagers did not exist as a group with ideas and fashions of their own until the 1950s.
- People in the 20th century have caused more pollution and environmental damage than all humans previously.

← Where was the 'global village'?

Everywhere! The name was invented by Canadian writer Marshall McLuhan (1911–80) to describe the worldwide information network created by 20th-century communications, such as the telephone, radio and films. He claimed that shared information and entertainment brought everyone closer together, wherever they lived!

INTERNET LINK
Find out about the first Moon landing
kids.msfc.nasa.gov/news/1999
/news%2Dapollo11.asp

Index

Quick Quiz answers

Page 5
1. Wiltshire
2. In caves in France and Spain
3. Europe, Africa and Asia

Page 11
1. Bath
2. The Colosseum
3. The city of Rome

Page 15
1. Bows and arrows
2. Agra
3. True

Page 23
1. St. Paul's Cathedral (built 1675–1710)
2. Henry VIII (1491–1547)
3. Henry VIII (in 1534)

Page 29
1. All of them! Steam train (1804), bicycle (1839), telephone (1876) electric light (1879)
2. Wilbur and Orville Wright (1903)
3. India

Page 31
1. Battle of the Somme (France, 1916)

2. John Logie Baird
3. 1972